THE TREE OF LIFE

A BOOK DEPICTING THE LIFE OF

CHARLES DARWIN

NATURALIST, GEOLOGIST & THINKER

BY

PETER SÍS

FRANCES FOSTER BOOKS

FARRAR STRAUS GIROUX

NEW YORK

AUTHOR'S NOTE

Charles Darwin regretted that he hadn't learned to draw. Instead, he kept
detailed descriptions of everything he saw. It is these dense and vivid written
passages in his diaries, letters, and journals that have inspired me to use my own
drawings, based on contemporary sources, to tell this story of his life. The text
in my visualization of Darwin's diary entries has been freely condensed from his
various writings about the voyage of the *Beagle*. Other sources for quotations and
information include Darwin's autobiography, his letters, and the first edition of
On the Origin of Species.

With thanks to Professor Peter Galison of Harvard University and Dr. Eric Korn
for their critical help in the making of this book.

The explanation of Darwin's theory of evolution is adapted
from *Charles Darwin* by Margaret J. Anderson and used by permission of
Enslow Publishers, Inc. All rights reserved.

Copyright © 2003 by Peter Sís
All rights reserved
Printed and bound in China by South China Printing Co. Ltd.
Designed by Robbin Gourley, Jennifer Crilly, and Barbara Grzeslo
First edition, 2003
1 3 5 7 9 10 8 6 4 2

Library of Congress Cataloging-in-Publication Data
Sís, Peter.
 The tree of life : a book depicting the life of Charles Darwin : naturalist, geologist &
thinker / by Peter Sís.— 1st ed.
  p. cm.
 Summary: Presents the life of the famous nineteenth-century naturalist using text from
Darwin's writings and detailed drawings by Sís.
 ISBN 0-374-45628-3
 1. Darwin, Charles, 1809-1882—Juvenile literature. [1. Darwin, Charles, 1809-1882.
2. Naturalists.] I. Title.

QH31.D2 S57 2003
576.8'092—dc21
[B]
                                            2002040706

Charles Darwin opens his eyes for the first time!

He has no idea that he will (a) start a revolution when he grows up, (b) sail around the world
on a five-year voyage, (c) spend many years studying nature, and (d) write a book that will change the
world. Luckily, he is unaware that (e) not everyone will see things his way, and that (f) he himself
will have doubts about revealing his grand conclusions.
Here is his story.

Both grandfathers were original thinkers and friends and members of . . .

Anti-slavery movement

Lunar Society

ERASMUS DARWIN

JOSIAH WEDGWOOD

Grandfather: doctor, philosopher, poet, who wrote about evolution in Zoonomia

Grandfather: a famous potter

Wedgwood vase

Father: doctor

Mother

ROBERT WARING DARWIN

SUSANNAH WEDGWOOD

THE MOUNT—Darwin's family home

Dies when Charles is eight

MARIANNE·CAROLINE SARAH·EMILY CATHERINE·SUSAN ELIZABETH·ERASMUS

Dr. Darwin wants the best for his children. He wants to give his sons, Erasmus and Charles, the kind of education that will prepare them to be gentlemen. They should be taught the classics. They should learn Greek and Latin. They should be able to read Homer and Virgil. They should study ancient history.

Charles sees things his own way.

I have never flogged the same boy twice in a week

DR. BUTLER, headmaster

SHREWSBURY SCHOOL

Charles and Erasmus's garden chemistry lab

When Charles is nine, his father sends him to join his brother at the nearby boarding school. It is a good school, strictly run in the style of its time.

Charles doesn't like the school. He doesn't like the classics. He doesn't like sleeping in a huge dormitory full of boys. He wants to be outdoors, riding, shooting, fishing, taking long walks through the countryside collecting things. He runs home whenever he can. He likes doing chemistry experiments in the toolshed at The Mount with his brother, Erasmus (Ras). Charles's friends nickname Charles "Gas."

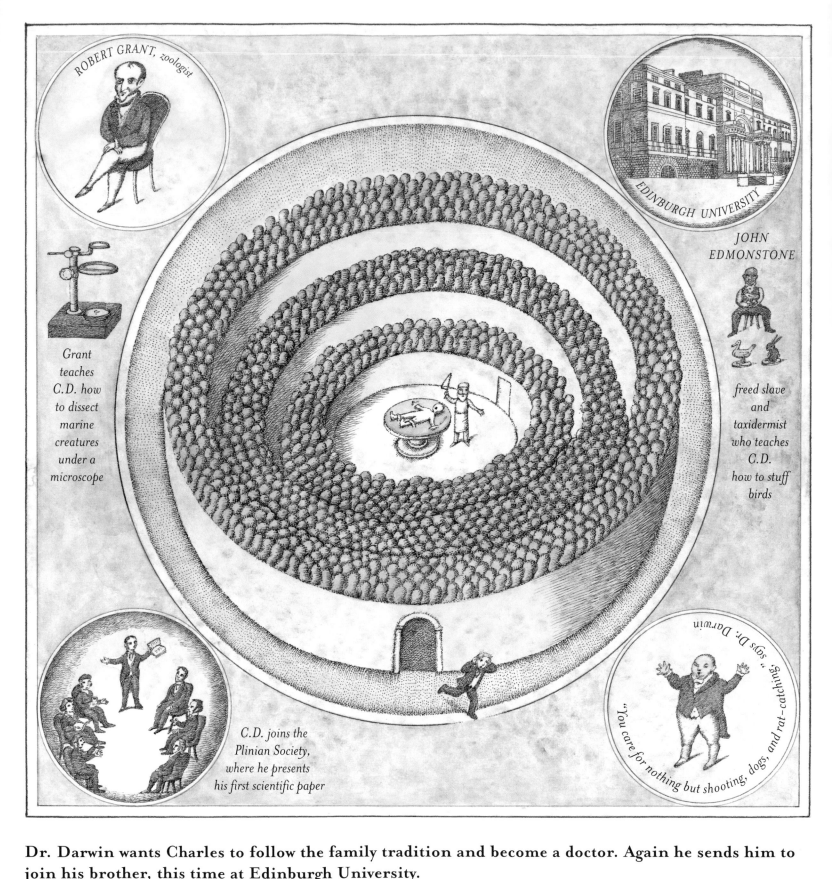

ROBERT GRANT, *zoologist*

EDINBURGH UNIVERSITY

JOHN EDMONSTONE

Grant teaches C.D. how to dissect marine creatures under a microscope

freed slave and taxidermist who teaches C.D. how to stuff birds

C.D. joins the Plinian Society, where he presents his first scientific paper

"You care for nothing but shooting, dogs, and rat-catching," says Dr. Darwin

Dr. Darwin wants Charles to follow the family tradition and become a doctor. Again he sends him to join his brother, this time at Edinburgh University.

Charles is sixteen. He likes the excitement of the big city, but he finds the medical lectures dull. He cannot bear to watch surgery, especially when it is performed on a child without anesthesia, which is not yet used. He prefers the natural sciences—geology, zoology, botany. He still likes riding, shooting, and collecting. Charles doesn't want to be a doctor and leaves Edinburgh after two years.

His father accuses him of wasting his time.

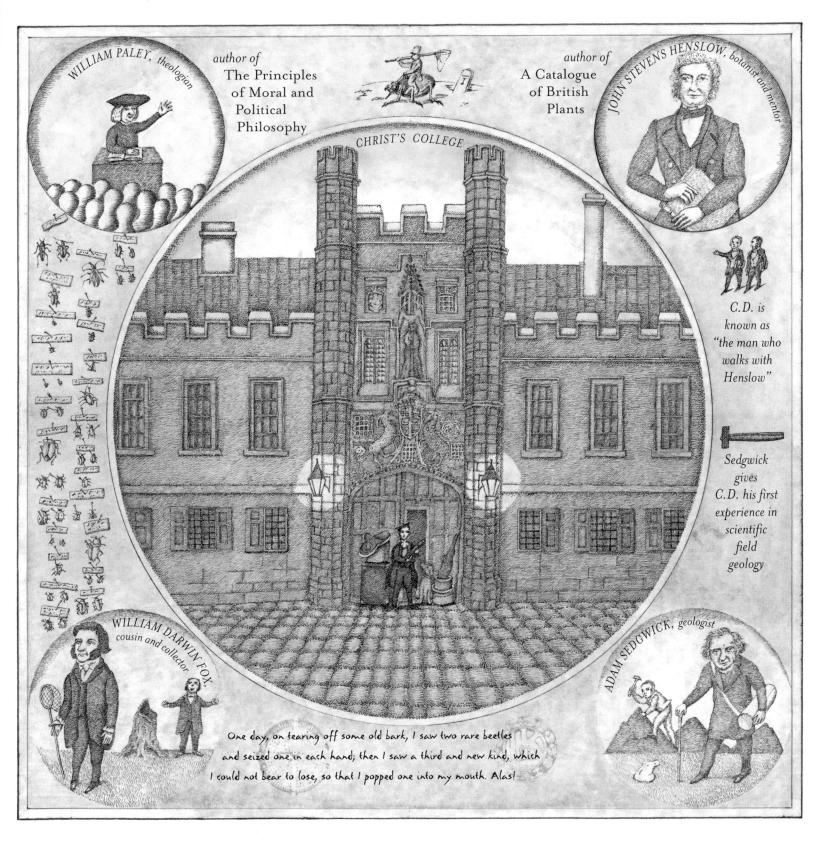

WILLIAM PALEY, *theologian*

author of
The Principles
of Moral and
Political
Philosophy

author of
A Catalogue
of British
Plants

JOHN STEVENS HENSLOW, *botanist and mentor*

CHRIST'S COLLEGE

C.D. is
known as
"the man who
walks with
Henslow"

Sedgwick
gives
C.D. his first
experience in
scientific
field
geology

WILLIAM DARWIN FOX,
cousin and collector

ADAM SEDGWICK, *geologist*

One day, on tearing off some old bark, I saw two rare beetles
and seized one in each hand; then I saw a third and new kind, which
I could not bear to lose, so that I popped one into my mouth. Alas!

Dr. Darwin comes up with an emergency plan. Charles will become a clergyman with a nice parsonage in the countryside. He will go to Christ's College at Cambridge University, where Erasmus had also studied. First Charles has to be tutored, to brush up on his Latin and Greek.

Charles doesn't care for his studies at Cambridge. He finds other lectures that interest him and attends those instead—in particular botany professor John Stevens Henslow's. He still likes his shooting and riding and is passionate about beetle collecting. When it comes time to take his final exams, he pleases his father by working hard and passing with high marks. Then he goes off on a geological walking trip through Wales, dreaming about an expedition to the Canary Islands. He sees himself as a naturalist.

WHEN CHARLES RETURNS HOME
FROM WALES, A LETTER FROM
PROFESSOR HENSLOW AWAITS
HIM WITH AN OFFER TO JOIN
THE VOYAGE OF THE *BEAGLE*.

AUGUST 24, 1831—THE OFFER
I have been asked . . . to recommend a naturalist as companion to
Capt FitzRoy employed by Government to survey the S. extremity of
America.—I have stated that I considered you to be the best qualified
person I know of who is likely to undertake such a situation— I state
this not on the supposition of y^r being a *finished* Naturalist, but as amply
qualified for collecting, observing, & noting any thing worthy to be
noted in natural History.

FATHER'S OBJECTIONS
(as relayed by Charles to his Uncle Josiah Wedgwood)

1) Disreputable to my character as a Clergyman
hereafter
2) A wild scheme
3) That they must have offered to many others
before me the place of Naturalist
4) And from its not being accepted there must
be some serious objection to the vessel or
expedition
5) That I should never settle down to a steady
life hereafter
6) That my accommodations would be most
uncomfortable
7) That you [Father] should consider it as again
changing my profession
8) That it would be a useless undertaking

On the last day of August I went to Maer [the Wedgwood family
home] where everything soon bore a different appearance. I found
every member of the family so strongly on my side, that
I determined to make another effort.

DARWIN'S ANSWER

My dear Sir . . . As far as my own mind is concerned, I should I think, certainly most gladly have accepted the opportunity, which you so kindly have offered me.—But my Father, although he does not decidedly refuse me, gives such strong advice against going,—that I should not be comfortable, if I did not follow it.

Uncle Jos persuaded Dr. Darwin to give his consent.

PRACTICAL ARRANGEMENTS

£500 for a place on the *Beagle*
£30 a year for expenses
Microscope
Geological compass
Telescope
Case of good strong pistols
Excellent rifle
Light walking shoes
Book on taxidermy
Humboldt's *Travels* (parting gift
from Henslow)
Lyell's *Principles of Geology*, vol. 1
(gift from FitzRoy)
Milton's *Paradise Lost*
Bible
Binoculars
Geological magnifying glass
Jars of spirits for preserving specimens

*September 5, 1831
Meeting FitzRoy in London*

TO R. W. DARWIN—AUGUST 31, 1831

My dear Father

I am afraid I am going to make you again very uncomfortable.—But upon consideration, I think you will excuse me once again stating my opinions on the offer of the Voyage . . .

I have given Uncle Jos, what I fervently trust is an accurate & full list of your objections, & he is kind enough to give his opinion on all.— The list & his answers will be enclosed.— But may I beg of you one favor . . . it will be doing me the greatest kindness, if you will send me a decided answer, yes or no.

... His Majesty's ship Beagle sailed from Devonport on the 27th of December, 1831.

ROBERT FITZROY

Captain; 26 years old
Grandson of Duke of Grafton
Royal Naval College at age 14
Command of Beagle at age 23

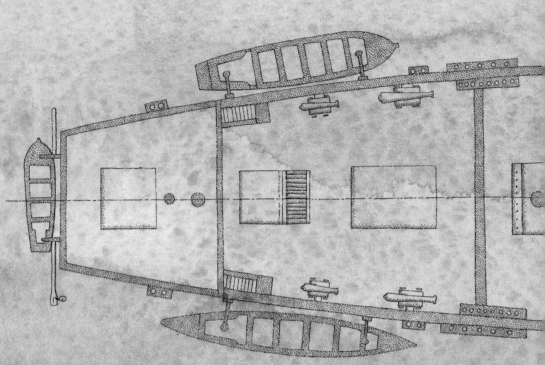

Sailed past Madeira because of heavy seas and turned away from Tenerife because of cholera quarantine—You may nearly guess at our disappointment.

I find to my great surprise that a ship is singularly comfortable for all sorts of work. Everything is so close at hand, & being cramped, makes one so methodical, that in the end I have been a gainer.

January 1832. Cape Verde Islands; 23 days at anchor. Geologising in a volcanic country is most delightful.

Crossing the equator

H.M.S. *BEAGLE* · 242 TONS · 90

MISSION: TO CHART THE SOUTHERN

CHRONOLOGICAL RECKONINGS AROUND

Breakfast with Captain—8 a.m.
Dissecting, classifying, making notes
Lunch—rice, peas, bread & water—1 p.m.
More studies, reading
Supper—meat, and foods to combat scurvy:
pickles, dried apples & lemon juice—5 p.m.

CHARLES DARWIN

Naturalist; 22 years old
As a civilian on the Royal Navy ship,
Darwin was not in uniform.
He wore the clothes
of a gentleman.

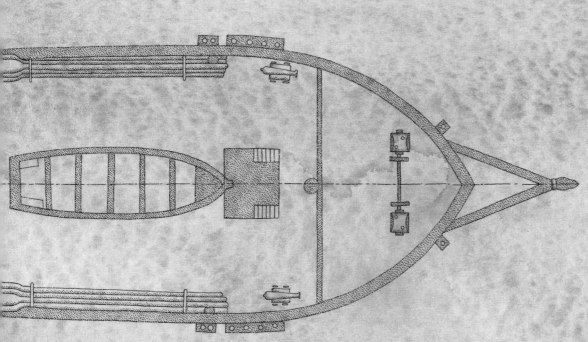

The misery I endured from sea-sickness is far far beyond
what I ever guessed . . . I found nothing but lying in my hammock did me
any good.— I must especially except [the] receipt of raisins, which is the
only food that the stomach will bear . . .

February 1832. St. Paul's Rocks.
Small archipelago 600 miles
off coast of Brazil

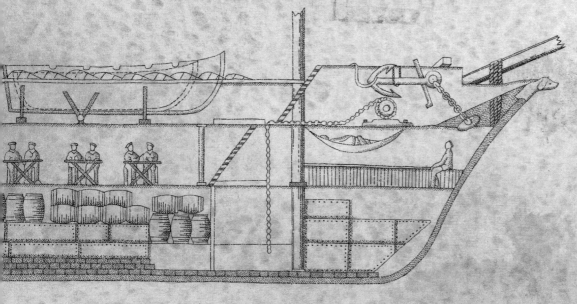

63 days out from England . . .
Bahia (Salvador), Brazil

FEET · 74 PEOPLE (PASSENGERS AND CREW)

COAST OF SOUTH AMERICA, AND TO MAKE
THE GLOBE TO DETERMINE THE LONGITUDE

Delight is a weak term to express the
feelings of a naturalist who, for
the first time, has been wandering by
himself in a Brazilian forest.

Ashore! Take quarters in town.

Ceiba trees, cabbage palms with Spanish moss, long rope-like lianas.

Join an Irishman, Patrick Lennon, to visit his coffee plantation.

Follow the coast, then inland to tropical rain forest.

Blue morpho butterfly.
Camphor-pepper-cinnamon-clove smell.

tiny hummingbirds

green parrots

toucans

nightly concert of frogs

epiphytic orchids sprouting from tree trunks

howler monkeys

monstrous anthills

Fight between *Pepsis* wasp and *Lycosa* spider.

lizards

snakes

Marching army of ants (black shining horde).

phasmid stick insect resembling twig of dry wood

A harmless moth disguises itself to look like a scorpion. A beetle assumes colors of poisonous fruit. Some moths have wings that imitate leaves, others have luminous false eyes.

APRIL. First attack of fever. First encounter with slavery. Brazilian soldiers ambush runaway slaves.

LENNON'S COFFEE PLANTATION—a quadrangle of thatched huts: master's quarters, stables, storehouses, slaves' quarters.

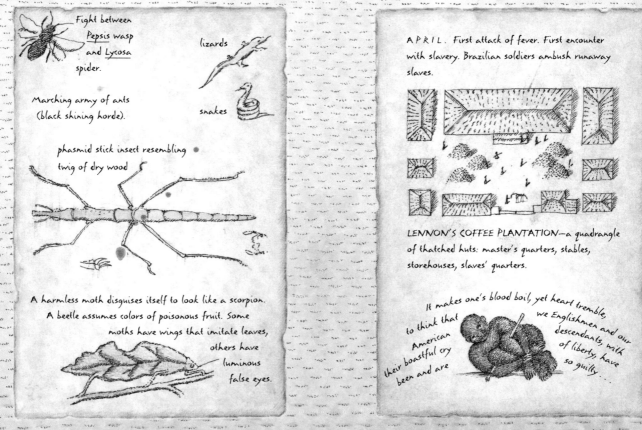

It makes one's blood boil, yet heart tremble, to think that American their boastful cry been and are we Englishmen and our descendants, with of liberty, have so guilty...

JUNE. Packing specimens to send to Henslow:

- spiders
- butterflies
- birds
- seashells
- glowworms
- bearded monkeys
- green parrots

68 species of a particularly minute beetle

JULY. Snipe-shooting party from the Beagle felled by fever. Three men have died. Much sea-sickness.

flying fish—porpoises

Anchored in estuary of Río Plata.
St. Elmo's fire lit up the mastheads and the rigging.
Penguins left long phosphorescent trails.

Cool temperatures. Growing a beard.

Eagerly awaiting arrival of the second volume of Lyell's *Principles of Geology*.

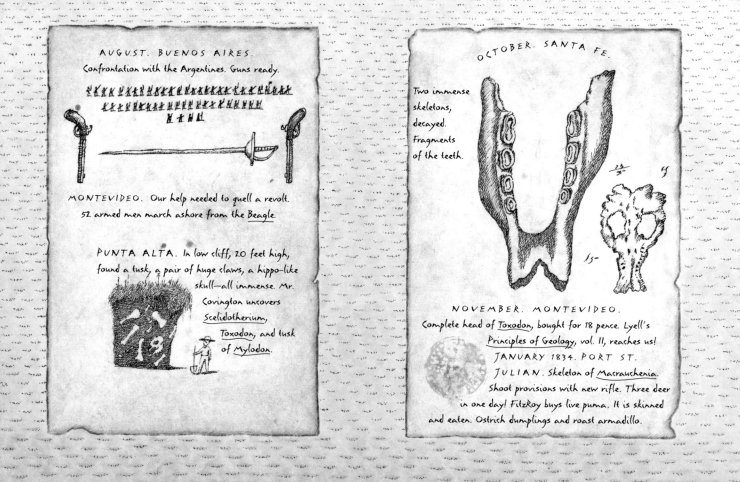

AUGUST. BUENOS AIRES.
Confrontation with the Argentines. Guns ready.

MONTEVIDEO. Our help needed to quell a revolt. 52 armed men march ashore from the Beagle.

PUNTA ALTA. In low cliff, 20 feet high, found a tusk, a pair of huge claws, a hippo-like skull—all immense. Mr. Covington uncovers *Scelidotherium*, *Toxodon*, and tusk of *Mylodon*.

OCTOBER. SANTA FE.

Two immense skeletons, decayed. Fragments of the teeth.

NOVEMBER. MONTEVIDEO.
Complete head of *Toxodon*, bought for 18 pence. Lyell's *Principles of Geology*, vol. II, reaches us!
JANUARY 1834. PORT ST. JULIAN. Skeleton of *Macrauchenia*. Shoot provisions with new rifle. Three deer in one day! FitzRoy buys live puma. It is skinned and eaten. Ostrich dumplings and roast armadillo.

LAND OF FIRE — TIERRA DEL FUEGO

DECEMBER 1832.
Cold, bleak land. Natives burn fires night and day. Paint faces, shave eyebrows and beards with sharp shells. Go naked except for mantle of guanaco skin over shoulders. Grease bodies and sleep on wet, near-frozen ground.

JEMMY BUTTON   FUEGIA BASKET   YORK MINSTER

On an earlier voyage Captain FitzRoy had taken some Fuegians back to London, named and educated them, and presented them at court. The Beagle was charged with returning them to their homeland, accompanied by a missionary, to civilize others. Crowds of Fuegians greet us.

Sailors unload goods for the mission—chamber pots, tea sets, linens, and china. Build a thatched hut, plant vegetable gardens, then sail off with the Beagle to explore, leaving Missionary Matthews alone with the Fuegians.

We return in nine days to find mission in chaos.

1833. FitzRoy buys ship Adventure f £1,300—no time to consult with Admir Ships carry out survey while I am in Maldonado, east of Montevideo. Two-week trip as far as river Polanc Travel with two armed men and twelve horses.
The only law here is the law of the gun.

Back in Maldonado, spend several weeks sorting out bones, rocks, plants, birds. JULY 24, 1833. Picked up by Beagle and sail for El Carmen on Río Negro.

AUGUST. Explore the pampas with English trader, guide, and escort of five gauchos.

Meet General Rosas— hired by Argentinian government to exterminate the Indians. I am a witness but can do nothing.

Observe Struthio Rhea—flock of ostriches swimming across river. Several hens use same nest. Sometimes 70 eggs, usually 20 to 30. The cock does the sitting and hatching.

RHEA DARWINII
(Avestruz Petise)

Hear of a very rare ostrich—Avestru Petise—darker, smaller, its eggs differen shaped and tinged with pale blue.

PORT DESIRE, PATAGONIA
Mr. Martens shot an ostrich; and I looked at it, forgetting at the moment, the most unaccountable manner, the wh subject of the Petises, and thought it wa a two-third grown one of the common sort. The bird was cooked and eaten before my memory returned. Fortunate the head, neck, legs, wings, many of th larger feathers, and a large part of the skin, had been   preserved From these a   very near perfect   specimen has been put together.

Eagles, vultures, zorillos (skunks), armadillos (good when roasted), partridges, black-necked swans, flamingos

Camping on open plains— saddles for pillows. Gauchos hunt with bolas: two or three stones tied to end of leather thongs are whirled around and hurled at an animal so legs become entangled. One day as I was amusing myself by galloping and whirling the balls round my head, I gave great pleasure to the gauchos by bringing down my own horse and myself with it.

AUGUST. Back to Punta Alta, where we found fossils a year ago. We now discovered a skeleton the size of a horse, carefully excavated it from the cliff face, labeled and catalogued the bones, and packed them for shipment home.

BUENOS AIRES — Spanish ladie
SEPTEMBER. Not a 60,000 inhabita pleasant place.

SHOPPING LIST
Paper, scissors, watch mended, spurs French dentist?, cigars.
Animals without tail, bookseller.
Writing home for four pairs of very str shoes, new lenses for microscope, book

Two petty officers from Beagle deserted. My Spanish is improving; in excellent health.

Trip to Santa Fe—300 miles up Paraná River. In northern pampas ride breast-high   in giant thistles.

Santa Fe governor hunts Indians for sport.

Down with fever. Hands black with mosquitoes.

Leaving horses with Covington—travel downriver by boat. In Las Conchas, surrounded by armed men. A revolution has broken out. I claim to know General Rosas. Slip away to Montevideo to   catch up with the Beagle.   Survey is all but done.

DECEMBER 6.
Beagle and Adventure leave.

CHRISTMAS DAY 1833—PORT DESIRE, PATAGONIA.
Shot a fine large guanaco. Contests of wrestling, jumping, running.

MARCH 1834.
Down to Tierra del Fuego for last call on Jemmy Button. Near the mission, a canoe comes   alongside with Jemmy   Button!

He no longer wore clothes. His hair wild. Brings presents—otter skins for FitzRoy and spearheads for me. Last we saw of him— lonely figure waving.

Channel about one and a half miles wide, hills on both sides about 2,000 feet high— scenery very retired . . .

Jackass penguin

MARCH 1834.
We reach Falkland Islands.

Falkland fox in great numbers

APRIL.
Back to Patagonia, Río Santa Cruz, to beach _Beagle_ for repairs. FitzRoy leads an expedition up the river with three weeks' provisions, three whale boats—25 men pulling boats upstream.
17 days upstream— 140 miles from sea.

Guanacos, pumas, condors: eight-foot wingspan

JUNE. Sail through Strait of Magellan to Pacific. Ice storms follow us to Chile. Mr. Hellyer had drowned in the Falklands, attempting to get a bird he had shot. Now Mr. Rowlett the purser dies and is buried at sea.

JULY 22, 1834.
Arrive at Valparaiso. Receive letters from home,

walking shoes,

and Lyell's _Geology_, vol. III.

Taking quarters with Richard Corfield, an old schoolfellow.

Expeditions into the Andes. 12,000 feet. See a bed of fossil shells. A forest of snow-white petrified trees—pines once on the shores of Atlantic, now 700 miles away. Then sunk beneath the sea, then raised 7,000 feet. It is sublime, like hearing a chorus of the _Messiah_ with full orchestra.

Admiralty in London does not approve purchase of _Adventure_. It is sold for £1,400.

NOVEMBER 21.
Anchor in bay of San Carlos, island of Chiloé.

Kill a Chilotan fox with geological hammer.

JANUARY 18, 1835.
Volcano Osorno, one hundred miles inland, erupts.

EARTHQUAKE! FEBRUARY 20, 1835. While Covington taking rest in apple orchard, earth trembles.

An enormous wall of water has hit the coast near Concepción.

The shore covered with debris—as if thousand great ships had been wrecked.

A moving hill of water swept into the bay. Then a second and third, each larger than previous ones. Ocean boiling.

Town of Concepción demolished in seconds.

Cathedral's walls fractured and roof caved in—a grand pile of ruins. Aftershocks for a week.

Elevations of the coast of Chile

MARCH–APRIL 1835.
Cross the Andes by the most lofty route, the Portillo Pass.

Two guides, ten mules, and mare with bell around neck. In high spirits after this 24-day trip. Never did I more deeply enjoy an equal space of time.

See Chilean miners, each carrying 200 pounds. I am appalled at their conditions.

Am attacked by the bloodsucking benchuca bug— a soft wingless black insect about an inch long. It is most disgusting.

Caught and kept one for four months. My illness last year may have been caused by the bite of this insect.

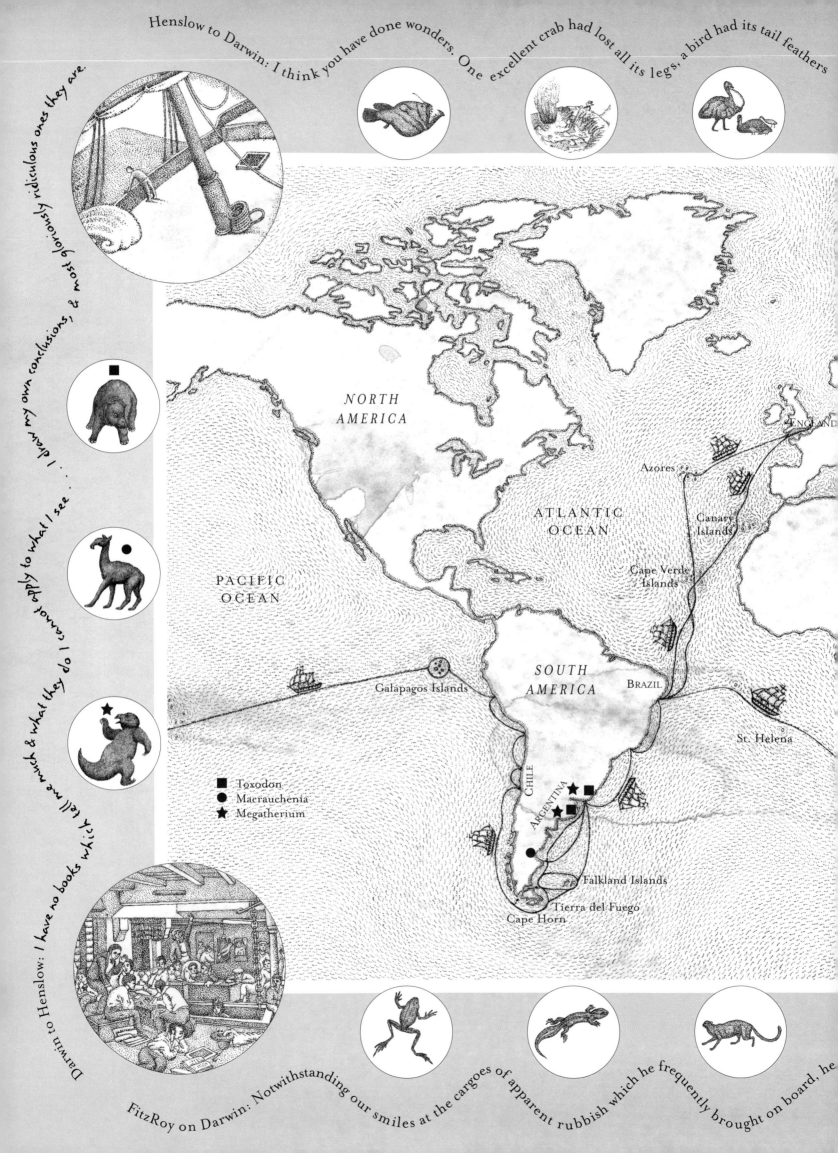

Darwin to Henslow: I have no books which tell me much & what they do I cannot apply to what I see . . . I draw my own conclusions, & most gloriously ridiculous ones they are.

NORTH
AMERICA

ENGLAND

Azores

ATLANTIC
OCEAN

Canary
Islands

Cape Verde
Islands

PACIFIC
OCEAN

Galápagos Islands

SOUTH
AMERICA

BRAZIL

St. Helena

■ Toxodon
● Macrauchenia
★ Megatherium

CHILE

ARGENTINA

Falkland Islands

Tierra del Fuego

Cape Horn

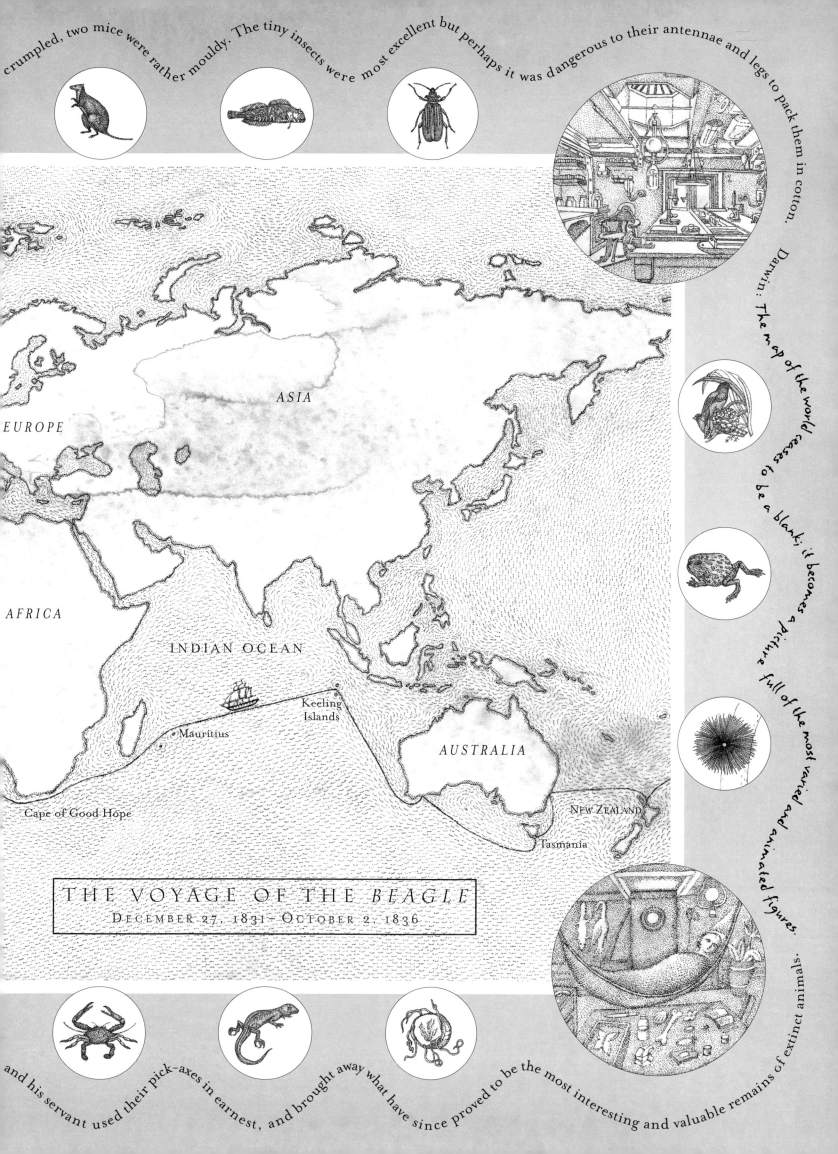

crumpled, two mice were rather mouldy. The tiny insects were most excellent but perhaps it was dangerous to their antennae and legs to pack them in cotton.

EUROPE

ASIA

AFRICA

INDIAN OCEAN

Keeling
Islands

Mauritius

Cape of Good Hope

AUSTRALIA

NEW ZEALAND

Tasmania

THE VOYAGE OF THE *BEAGLE*
DECEMBER 27, 1831 – OCTOBER 2, 1836

Darwin: The map of the world ceases to be a blank; it becomes a picture full of the most varied and animated figures.

and his servant used their pick-axes in earnest, and brought away what have since proved to be the most interesting and valuable remains of extinct animals.

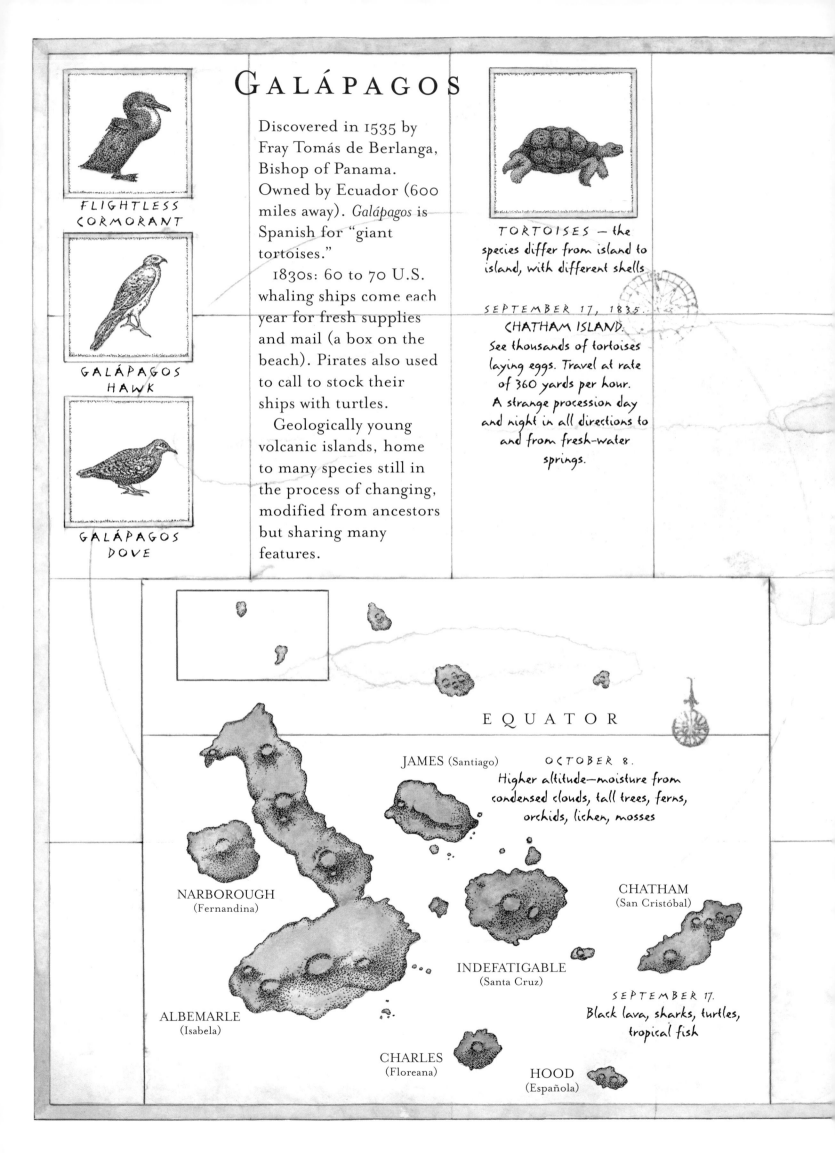

GALÁPAGOS

Discovered in 1535 by Fray Tomás de Berlanga, Bishop of Panama. Owned by Ecuador (600 miles away). *Galápagos* is Spanish for "giant tortoises."

1830s: 60 to 70 U.S. whaling ships come each year for fresh supplies and mail (a box on the beach). Pirates also used to call to stock their ships with turtles.

Geologically young volcanic islands, home to many species still in the process of changing, modified from ancestors but sharing many features.

FLIGHTLESS CORMORANT

GALÁPAGOS HAWK

GALÁPAGOS DOVE

TORTOISES — the species differ from island to island, with different shells

SEPTEMBER 17, 1835.
CHATHAM ISLAND.
See thousands of tortoises laying eggs. Travel at rate of 360 yards per hour. A strange procession day and night in all directions to and from fresh-water springs.

EQUATOR

JAMES (Santiago)

OCTOBER 8.
Higher altitude—moisture from condensed clouds, tall trees, ferns, orchids, lichen, mosses

NARBOROUGH
(Fernandina)

CHATHAM
(San Cristóbal)

INDEFATIGABLE
(Santa Cruz)

ALBEMARLE
(Isabela)

SEPTEMBER 17.
Black lava, sharks, turtles, tropical fish

CHARLES
(Floreana)

HOOD
(Española)

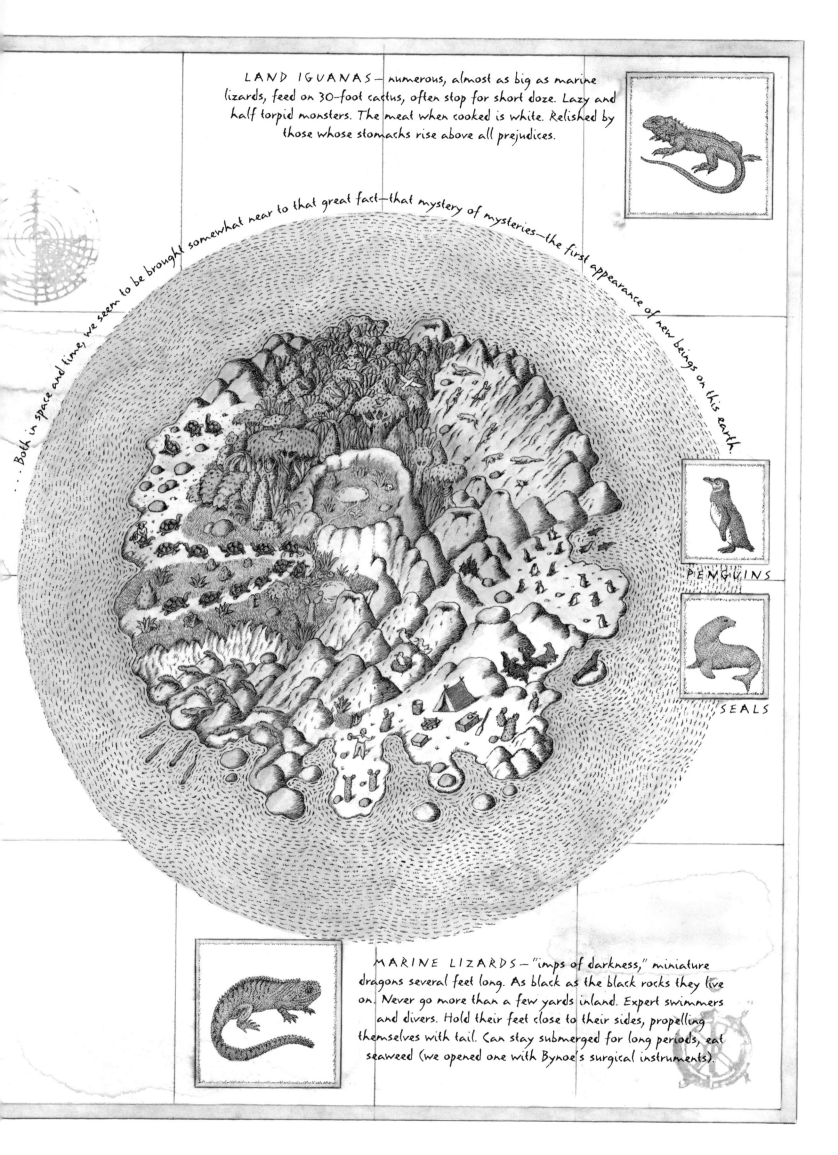

LAND IGUANAS — numerous, almost as big as marine lizards, feed on 30-foot cactus, often stop for short doze. Lazy and half torpid monsters. The meat when cooked is white. Relished by those whose stomachs rise above all prejudices.

...Both in space and time, we seem to be brought somewhat near to that great fact—that mystery of mysteries—the first appearance of new beings on this earth.

PENGUINS

SEALS

MARINE LIZARDS — "imps of darkness," miniature dragons several feet long. As black as the black rocks they live on. Never go more than a few yards inland. Expert swimmers and divers. Hold their feet close to their sides, propelling themselves with tail. Can stay submerged for long periods, eat seaweed (we opened one with Bynoe's surgical instruments).

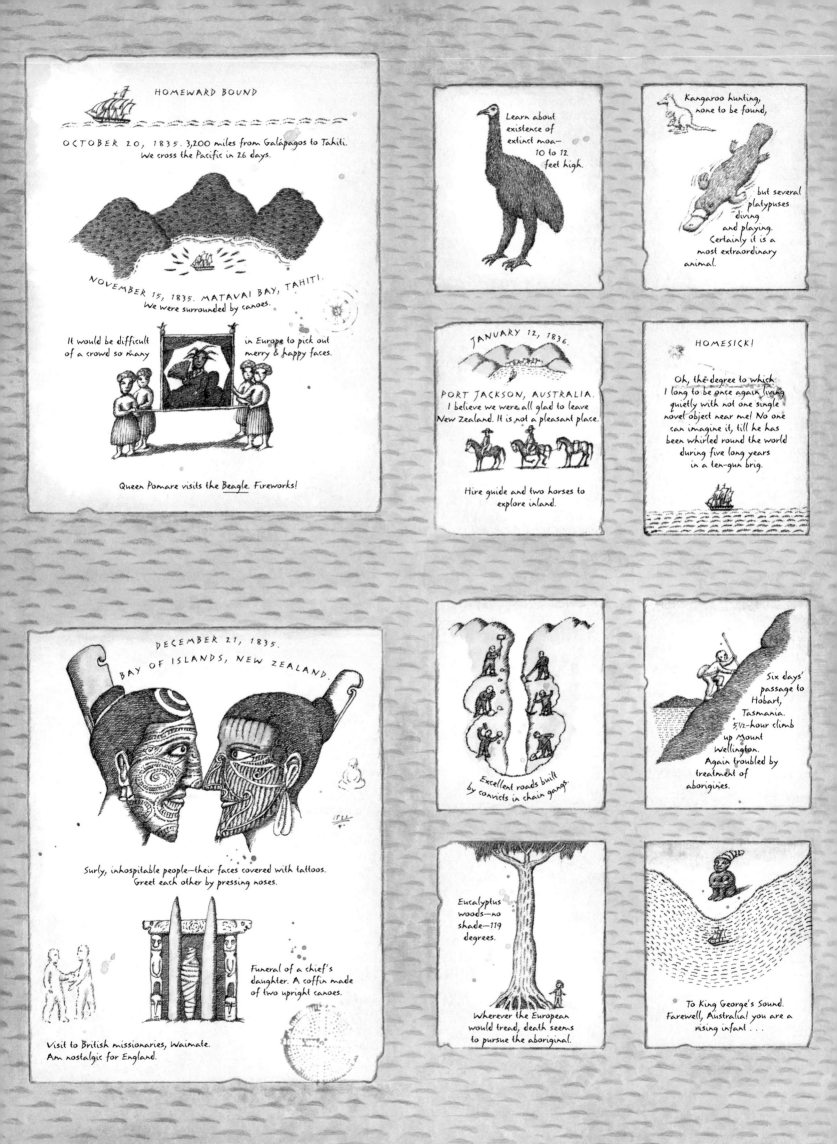

HOMEWARD BOUND

OCTOBER 20, 1835. 3,200 miles from Galápagos to Tahiti. We cross the Pacific in 26 days.

NOVEMBER 15, 1835. MATAVAI BAY, TAHITI. We were surrounded by canoes.

It would be difficult in Europe to pick out of a crowd so many merry & happy faces.

Queen Pomare visits the Beagle. Fireworks!

DECEMBER 21, 1835. BAY OF ISLANDS, NEW ZEALAND.

Surly, inhospitable people—their faces covered with tattoos. Greet each other by pressing noses.

Funeral of a chief's daughter. A coffin made of two upright canoes.

Visit to British missionaries, Waimate. Am nostalgic for England.

Learn about existence of extinct moa— 10 to 12 feet high.

Kangaroo hunting, none to be found, but several platypuses diving and playing. Certainly it is a most extraordinary animal.

JANUARY 12, 1836.

PORT JACKSON, AUSTRALIA. I believe we were all glad to leave New Zealand. It is not a pleasant place.

Hire guide and two horses to explore inland.

HOMESICK!

Oh, the degree to which I long to be once again living quietly with not one single novel object near me! No one can imagine it, till he has been whirled round the world during five long years in a ten-gun brig.

Excellent roads built by convicts in chain gangs.

Six days' passage to Hobart, Tasmania. 5½-hour climb up Mount Wellington. Again troubled by treatment of aborigines.

Eucalyptus woods—no shade—119 degrees.

Wherever the European would tread, death seems to pursue the aboriginal.

To King George's Sound. Farewell, Australia! you are a rising infant . . .

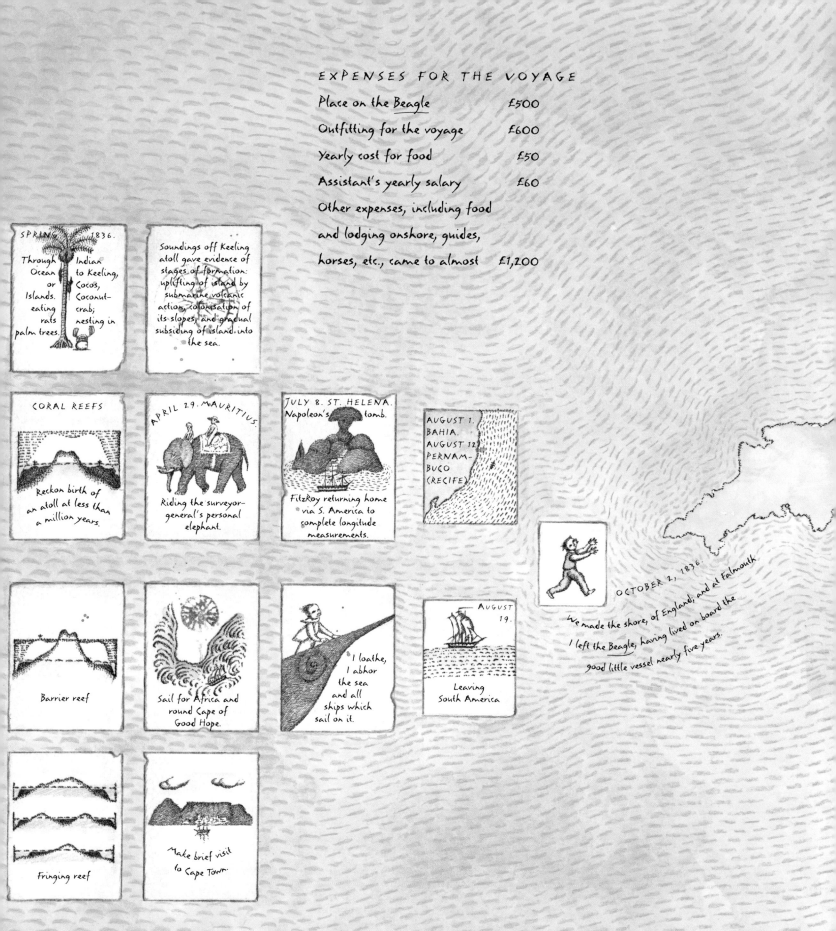

EXPENSES FOR THE VOYAGE

Place on the Beagle	£500
Outfitting for the voyage	£600
Yearly cost for food	£50
Assistant's yearly salary	£60
Other expenses, including food and lodging onshore, guides, horses, etc., came to almost	£1,200

SPRING 1836.

Through Indian Ocean to Keeling, or Cocos, Islands. Coconut-eating crab; rats nesting in palm trees.

Soundings off Keeling atoll gave evidence of stages of formation: uplifting of island by submarine volcanic action, colonisation of its slopes, and gradual subsiding of island into the sea.

CORAL REEFS

Reckon birth of an atoll at less than a million years.

APRIL 29. MAURITIUS.

Riding the surveyor-general's personal elephant.

JULY 8. ST. HELENA. Napoleon's tomb.

FitzRoy returning home via S. America to complete longitude measurements.

AUGUST 1. BAHIA. AUGUST 12. PERNAMBUCO (RECIFE).

OCTOBER 2, 1836. We made the shore of England; and at Falmouth I left the Beagle, having lived on board the good little vessel nearly five years.

Barrier reef

Sail for Africa and round Cape of Good Hope.

I loathe, I abhor the sea and all ships which sail on it.

AUGUST 19.

Leaving South America

Fringing reef

Make brief visit to Cape Town.

The voyage of the Beagle has been by far the most important event in my life and has determined my whole career . . . I owe to the voyage the first real training or education of my mind. I was led to attend closely to several branches of natural history, and thus my powers of observation were improved, though they were already fairly developed.

GALÁPAGOS FINCHES

JOHN GOULD
(ornithologist)

RICHARD OWEN
(zoologist)

GEORGE R. WATERHOUSE
(zoologist)

CHARLES LYELL
(geologist)

Reconstruction of Megatherium

JOSEPH DALTON HOOKER
(botanist)

LEONARD JENYNS
(ichthyologist)

THOMAS MALTHUS

An Essay on the Principle of Population

Charles and Emma's

Elected to the

On his return, Darwin set out on a course that became ever more divided into three distinct areas: public, private, and secret (his developing a theory about the evolution and adaptation of species).

PUBLIC LIFE: **Thanks to Henslow, who had published extracts from Darwin's letters, he was seen as England's most promising young geologist. He met his idol, Lyell, and worked furiously—writing, talking, meeting people. He distributed part of the specimens collected on his voyage to various experts to study and classify.**

PRIVATE LIFE: After spending some time at The Mount, he went to Cambridge, then to London.

SECRET LIFE: He analyzed what he had seen on his voyage and sketched in a notebook a tree showing old species branching into new ones. In 1838, he read Thomas Malthus's *Essay on the Principle of Population*. "Here, then, I had at last got a theory by which to work."

ORANGUTAN JENNY

Geological Society

Athenaeum Club
(same time as
Charles Dickens)

Reconstruction of Mylodon

Firstborn
WILLIAM ERASMUS

ANNE
ELIZABETH

Darwin's
Journal of Researches (1839)

The Zoology of
the "Beagle"
(1839–1843)

Marriage to
Emma Wedgwood
(1839)

London home

1837 sketch of the branching formation of genera—the tree of life

Royal Society (1839)

PUBLIC LIFE: The skeletons reconstructed from the fossil bones found in South America were put on exhibit and drew huge crowds. Darwin's books about the voyage were well received, and he was invited to join the most prestigious scientific societies and clubs.

PRIVATE LIFE: Approaching thirty, he contemplated the future and playfully drew up a balance sheet: to marry or not to marry. "My God, it is intolerable to think of spending one's whole life, like a neuter bee, working, working . . . living all one's days solitarily in smoky dirty London house.—Only picture to yourself a nice soft wife on a sofa with good fire, & books & music perhaps . . . Marry—marry—marry." He married his cousin Emma, and their first two children were born in London.

SECRET LIFE: He visited the zoo to see the new sensation, orangutan Jenny. "Man from monkeys?" he wrote in his notebook, thinking about his theory of the "transmutation"—evolution—of species in deep secret.

London 16 miles Downe

DOWN HOUSE

Downstairs

Tennis court

Worm Stone

EMMA
1808–1896

GEORGE HOWARD
1845–1912

WILLIAM ERASMUS
1839–1914

HENRIETTA EMMA
(ETTY)
1843–1930

Greenhouse

ANNE ELIZABETH
(ANNIE)
1841–1851

MARY ELEANOR
b. & d. 1842

Upstairs

PUBLIC LIFE: **Darwin threw himself into his work to forget his grief over the death of his third child. To FitzRoy, he wrote: "My life goes on like clockwork and I am fixed on the spot where I shall end it." He continued a prolific correspondence—writing and receiving more than 15,000 letters in his lifetime—exchanging ideas, mostly with men of science.**

PRIVATE LIFE: In 1842, the Darwins moved from London to Down House in the village of Downe in Kent. A daughter was born just days after they moved in, and died three weeks later. Darwin was grief-stricken. He constructed his "Sandwalk," on which he took his daily walks—thinking, thinking, thinking.

SECRET LIFE: He had to share his secret with somebody and chose Joseph Dalton Hooker. He also confessed to Emma. Then an anonymously published book, *Vestiges of the Natural History of Creation*, suggesting that people were descended from fish, created such an uproar that it sent Darwin back into hiding. He knew that his ideas might invite the same anti-evolutionary furor.

Groom

Butler

Gardeners

Cook and maids

Governess

LEONARD
1850–1943

FRANCIS (FRANK)
1848–1925

HORACE
1851–1928

CHARLES WARING
1856–1858

ELIZABETH
(LIZZIE, BESSY)
1847–1926

Sandwalk

1844 publication
of Vestiges

JOSEPH HOOKER
CHARLES LYELL
ASA GRAY

Still, he kept on researching and pondering. All of his previous reading, all of his studies, along with the reports from the scientists who were classifying his specimens, were coming together to help him shape his theory. He wrote to Hooker:

I have been now ever since my return engaged in a very presumptuous work & which I know no one individual who would not say a very foolish one.—I was so struck with distribution of Galapagos organisms, &c . . . that I determined to collect blindly every sort of fact, which could bear any way on what are species.—I have read heaps of agricultural & horticultural books, & have never ceased collecting facts— At last gleams of lights have come, & I am almost convinced (quite contrary to opinion I started with) that species are not (it is like confessing a murder) immutable . . . I think I have found out (here's presumption!) the simple way by which species become exquisitely adapted to various ends.—You will now groan, & think to yourself, "on what a man have I been wasting my time in writing to."—I should, five years ago, have thought so.

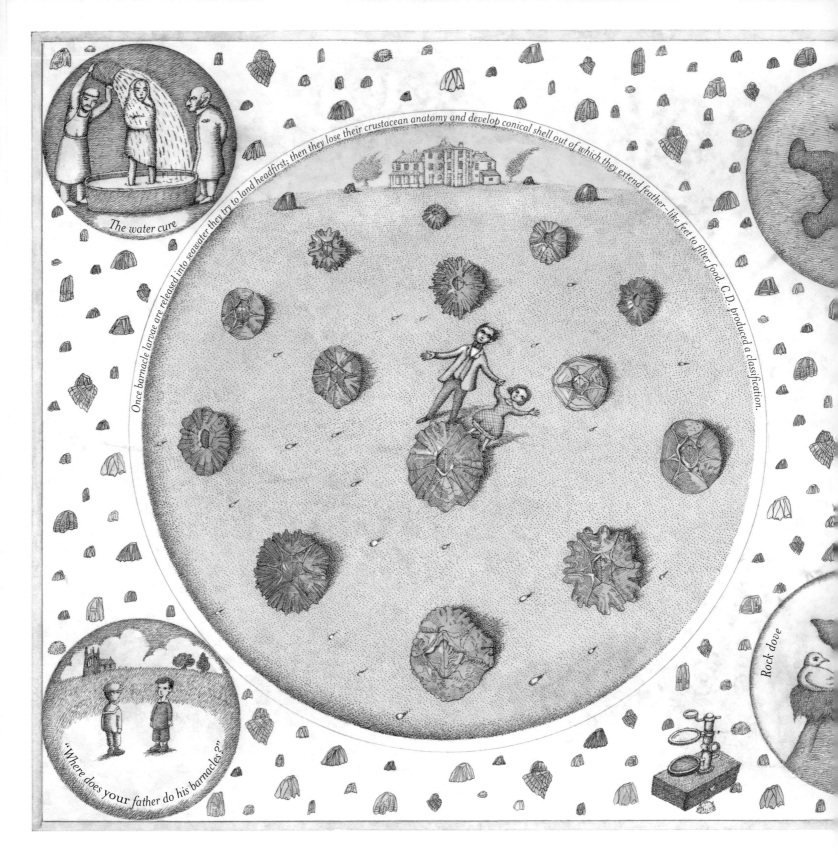

The water cure

Once barnacle larvae are released into seawater they try to land headfirst; then they lose their crustacean anatomy and develop conical shell out of which they extend feather-like feet to filter food. C.D. produced a classification.

"Where does your father do his barnacles?"

Rock dove

PUBLIC LIFE: **Darwin decided he needed to produce more work to be accepted as a first-class naturalist and planned to write a short paper on barnacles. He ended up spending the next eight years studying living and fossil barnacles. Then, in 1851–1854, he published four volumes on them. He won the recognition he was looking for and honors as well.**

PRIVATE LIFE: His work was interrupted by a long period of ill health, and in 1849 he took the then-popular water cure, which helped him. His favorite daughter, ten-year-old Annie, developed symptoms similar to his and died in 1851. Another son, Horace, was born three weeks later.

SECRET LIFE: His writings about evolution sat on the shelf.

ALFRED
RUSSEL WALLACE'S
manuscript came as a bombshell to
Darwin. His friends Lyell and Hooker
arranged for Wallace's paper, together with
a summary of Darwin's 1844 essay and outline
of his theory, to be presented to the Linnaean
Society on July 1, 1858. There was no reaction;
the president of the society called it an
uneventful year. Relieved, Darwin set to
work. Over the next eight months,
he wrote *On the Origin of
Species.*

CHARLES LYELL

THOMAS HENRY HUXLEY

JOSEPH DALTON HOOKER

LINNAEAN SOCIETY

On the Origin of Species sparked an explosion. Thomas Henry Huxley joined Lyell

...inhabitants of South America, and in the geolo...

Thus, from the war of nature, from famine and death, the most exalted ob...

When on board H.M.S. "Beagle," as naturalist, I was much struck with certain facts in the distribution of the inhabitants of South America, and in the geolo...

Darwin did not invent the idea of evolution. Others—Thales, Aristotle, de Buffon, Lamarck—had looked to fact rather than mythology to understand changes in the natural world. Darwin contributed the theory of natural selection backed up by evidence to show how evolution really worked.

DARWIN'S THEORY RESTS ON THREE MAIN POINTS: I. Plants and animals have m...

THE OR

BY MEANS

PRESERVATION OF F

BY CHA

FELLOW OF THE ROYA
AUTHOR OF 'JOURNAL OF

PUBLISHED NOV

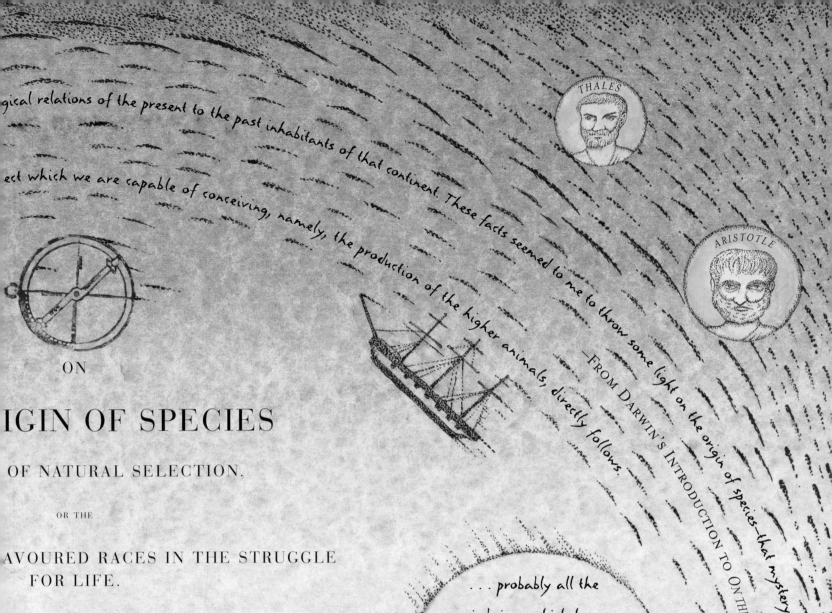

...gical relations of the present to the past inhabitants of that continent. These facts seemed to me to throw some light on the origin of species—that mystery of mysteries ...

...ect which we are capable of conceiving, namely, the production of the higher animals, directly follows.

—FROM DARWIN'S INTRODUCTION TO ON THE ORIGIN OF SPECIES

THALES

ARISTOTLE

ON

IGIN OF SPECIES

OF NATURAL SELECTION,

OR THE

AVOURED RACES IN THE STRUGGLE
FOR LIFE.

RLES DARWIN, M.A.,

L, GEOLOGICAL, LINNÆAN, ETC., SOCIETIES;
RESEARCHES DURING H. M. S. BEAGLE'S VOYAGE
ROUND THE WORLD.'

MBER 24, 1859, BY JOHN MURRAY, LONDON

... probably all the organic beings which have ever lived on this earth have descended from some one primordial form ... Light will be thrown on the origin of man and his history.

ore offspring than are needed to replace the parents. 2. The offspring of a set of parents are not all exactly alike.

CHARLES WARING DARWIN

ALFRED RUSSEL WALLACE, naturalist

Fleeing scarlet fever

PUBLIC LIFE: **Darwin became a pigeon breeder, hoping that by studying the variations in domesticated pigeons (descended from the rock dove) he might find clues to support his theory of adaptation to an environment and natural selection. He also did experiments with plants and seeds.**

PRIVATE LIFE: In 1858, his youngest son, Charles Waring, died of scarlet fever. The family fled Down House.

SECRET LIFE: On September 9, 1854, he wrote in his journal: "Began sorting notes for species theory." He dusted off his secret writings, took another look at an unpublished essay he had written in 1844 about the transmutation of species, and in 1857 wrote a letter to the American botanist Asa Gray, outlining his theory. Then, on June 18, 1858, he received a manuscript from Alfred Russel Wallace, a young botanist collecting specimens in the Malay archipelago, setting forth much the same conclusions as Darwin's about natural selection. Darwin turned to Lyell. He wrote, "Your words have come true with a vengeance that I should be forestalled . . ." Lyell and Hooker came up with a plan to establish Darwin's priority.

While Darwin's friends defended his theory of evolution by natural selection—especially T. H. Huxley, who was called "Darwin's bulldog"—Darwin kept on working. He was always puzzling over something—orchids, earthworms, facial expressions—and spent the next twenty years revising his earlier books and writing new ones.

1862 *On the Various Contrivances by Which British and Foreign Orchids Are Fertilised by Insects, and on the Good Effects of Intercrossing*

1865 *The Movements and Habits of Climbing Plants*

1868 *The Variation of Animals and Plants under Domestication*

1871 *The Descent of Man, and Selection in Relation to Sex*

1872 *The Expression of the Emotions in Man and Animals* (One of the first books illustrated with photographs; 5,267 copies sold in one day.)

1876 *The Effects of Cross and Self Fertilisation in the Vegetable Kingdom*

1881 *The Formation of Vegetable Mould, Through the Action of Worms, with Observations on Their Habits* (Horace Darwin designed a special instrument called the Worm Stone to measure the action of worms.)

My industry has been nearly as great as it could have been in the observation and collection of facts. What is far more important, my love of natural science has been steady and ardent . . . From my early youth I have had the strongest desire to understand or explain whatever I observed,—that is, to group all facts under some general laws.

Happy

Surprised

LINNAEUS

It may be said that natural selection is daily and hourly scrutinising, throughout the world, every variation, even the slightest, throughout the world, every variation, even the slightest; and that, whilst this planet has

There is grandeur in this view of life, with its several powers, having been originally breathed into a few forms or into one; and that, whilst this planet has

Life on earth has been generated over billions of years in a single branching tree—the Tree of Life . . .

3. The overall number of each kind of plant or animal mostly stays the same. The struggle for existence—natural s

... We see nothing of these slow changes in progress, until the hand of time has marked the long lapses of ages.

gone cycling on according to the fixed law of gravity, from so simple a beginning endless forms most beautiful and most wonderful have been, and are being, evolved.

ERASMUS DARWIN

Darwin did not say that God had not created life on earth. What he said was that creation did not happen all at once. Plants and animals change over time, and all are descended from similar species that lived long ago. This was supported by his studies of fossils.

election, or survival of the fittest—keeps the numbers down.

BISHOP SAMUEL WILBERFORCE

RICHARD OWEN

OXFORD DEBATE

and Hooker in support of Darwin, while Richard Owen led the opposition.

Sad

Angry

My habits are methodical, and this has been of not a little use for my particular line of work . . . I have had ample leisure from not having to earn my own bread. Even ill-health, though it has annihilated several years of my life, has saved me from the distractions of society and amusement.

Darwin's daily routine started with an early-morning walk and looked something like this:

7:45 a.m.	Breakfast by himself
8:00	Work (his most productive time)
9:30	Break (Emma reads letters to him)
10:30	Work
12:00 noon	Rain or shine, stroll around the Sandwalk with Polly, his dog, often stopping by the greenhouse to check his plant experiments
1:00 p.m.	Lunch (main meal)
1:30	Read the newspapers on the sofa in the drawing room
2:00	Sit in his big chair in the study by the fireplace and write letters
3:00	Rest in his bedroom while Emma reads letters or a novel to him
4:00	Late-afternoon stroll
4:30	Work
5:30	Rest; Emma reads to him
7:30	Light dinner with his family
8:00	Play backgammon with Emma
8:30	Read or study; listen to Emma play the piano or read a novel
10:00	Get ready for bed

As far as I can judge, I am not apt to follow blindly the lead of other men. I have steadily endeavoured to keep my mind free, so as to give up any hypothesis, however much beloved (and I cannot resist forming one on every subject), as soon as facts are shown to be opposed to it.

Charles Darwin died on April 19, 1882, and was buried in Westminster Abbey.

With his major books written and the children grown, Darwin, always in ill health, felt old and helpless.

Darwin, with the help of his family, carried out experiments to test the behavior of worms. They reacted to the vibrations of the piano.

"He moons about in the garden, and I have seen him standing doing nothing before a flower for ten minutes at a time. If he only had something to do, I really believe he would be better."
—Darwin's gardener

Darwin's funeral

ARISTOTLE

CARL LINNAEUS

J. B. LAMARCK

COMTE DE BUFFON

Paul Bright   Ben Cort

Good Books

Intercourse, PA 17534
800/762-7171
www.goodbks.com

Under the bed there's a smelly shoe,
A piece of jigsaw, green and blue,
Some purple pants, an apple core

. . . but under the bed there's

something more!

Under the bed there are bugs and beasts, nibbling crumbs for their

midnight feasts, gobbling, squabbling, all night through,
And much too busy
to think about you.

Under the bed is a dragon dozing,
One eye closed, the other closing,
Dreaming of mountains and morning dew,
And much too sleepy to think about you.

Under the bed is an alligator,
Who might be feeling hungry later.
He likes a pizza, or maybe two,
So I don't expect he'll be bothering you.

Under the bed is a grizzly bear
(Now, don't ask me how he got there),
Rolling and scratching, like grizzlies do,
And far too lazy to think about you.

But, under the bed
there's something more . . .
Something bigger than a stable door,
Horrible, hairy, with warts on his nose,
With knots in his tail, and mold on his toes,
With a big, big mouth and huge,
huge paws . . .

. . . though he's never been
known to show his claws.

He's under the bed
and he's sucking his thumb!
He calls for his daddy
or mommy to come!
And he says as he shakes
from his toes to his head:

"I saw something
frightening inside
the bed!"

And out of the room flee the bugs and beasts,
Scattering crumbs from their midnight feasts.
Out of the room flies the dragon dozing,
One eye open and the other one closing.

Out of the room crawls the alligator,
Who might be feeling hungry later.
Out of the room bounds the grizzly bear
(And don't ask me how he got there).

And out of the room runs something more,
Who trips on his tail as he gets to the door,
Who rolls down the stairs falling flat on his nose,
Bashing his bottom and banging his toes,
With a big, big mouth and huge, huge paws . . .
though he never showed even a glimpse
of his claws.
They all run out in a terrible stew,
For the frightening thing in the bed is . . .

YOU!

Now there's nobody under the bed
anymore. But you'd better just look,
to be perfectly sure!